Vespa

Vespa

Valerio Boni

Vespa

RIZZOLI
NEW YORK

Vespa

Text: Valerio Boni
Photographs: images in this volume are partly taken from the author's collection and partly from photographic album Vespa (art direction by Max Pinucci); for the other images, thanks are extended to the "Antonella Bechi Piaggio" historical archive.

The brand names "VESPA ®," "PIAGGIO ®," "CELLA ESAGONALE NUOVO LOGO ®," and "P PIAGGIO scudo e figura ®" are registered trademarks owned exclusively by Piaggio & C. S.p.A. Any unauthorized use is in breach of trademark copyright and other applicable laws.

Special thanks to Piaggio & C. S.p.A. and Fondazione Piaggio Onlus for their help in creating this book.

Layout: Zadig – Torino (Turin)
Prepress: gi.mac – Savigliano (CN)
Translation: Stephen Davies (Centro Traduzioni Imolese)

Editorial manager: Alberto Dragone
Editorial coordinator: Stefano Delmastro, Paola Morelli
Editorial assistant: Anna Gribaudo

The Editors have endeavored to trace the origin of photographs in this volume covered by copyright. Authors not identified or contacted are kindly requested to contact the publisher directly.

First published in the United States of America in 2007 by
Rizzoli International Publications, Inc.
300 Park Avenue South
New York, NY 10010
www.rizzoliusa.com

Originally published in Italy in 2006 by
Edizioni Gribaudo – Redazione Varia-Illustrati
Corso Roma 35 - Savigliano (CN)

©Edizioni Gribaudo srl
Savigliano (CN)

ISBN-10: 0-8478-2936-7
ISBN-13: 978-0-8478-2936-1

Library of Congress Control Number 2006933396

2007 2008 2009 2010 / 10 9 8 7 6 5 4 3 2 1

Printed in Italy by Grafiche Busti

Contents

Preface

Felice remembers it as the official escort of the Giro d'Italia (Italy's equivalent of the Tour de France). Altero recognizes it as his entire generation's object of desire. Franco retains a vivid memory of the moment in 1960 when he asked his friend to lend it to him and, instead of a riding around the block as usual, took off from Monza for Rome to see the Olympics. Luca will never forget when on a lark, he rode a thousand kilometers from Brussels to Milan under torrential rain. Little does it matter that their surnames were Gimondi, Matteoli, Varisco, Regondi, Rossi, or Bianchi, and that they were champions, ministers, bank clerks, photographers, students, or pensioners. In Italy, there are millions of people with fond memories linked to the Vespa. Because every family has, has had, or will have a Vespa.

We got ours on May 14, 1974, after I finally convinced my father to let me have the 162 thousand liras needed to purchase a purplish red R50. Very few of the world's products have survived sixty years of fast-changing fashion while managing to please everyone. And though it remains a jewel of design, a Vespa is still cheaper than a diamond. New or used, it is affordable to just about anyone. Those who have attempted to imitate it in the hope of obtaining similar success have been sorely disappointed. Stripping and analyzing every single nut and bolt has failed to reveal the secret of the Vespa's longevity.

Vespa is much more than a scooter. It has warded off attacks and weathered crises without ever changing its basic design—which even today, remains faithful to the one that debuted in 1946. If ever a time machine should be invented, it seems only fitting that it would have the irresistible lines of the Vespa.

Valerio Boni

Introduction

The first Vespas to hit the roads of Italy were, despite the country's critical economic situation, met with sardonic smiles. It was less than a year since the end of the Second World War, and new products that broke with tradition were not welcomed with the same spirit as they are today. Perhaps not too surprisingly, then, many predicted a quick demise for this odd little vehicle. Instead, the Vespa has remained faithful to the lines of its prototype throughout every stage of its evolution, has been manufactured by the millions, has traversed the streets of not only Italy but nearly every country in the world, and has proved adept at surviving economic crises and outliving passing trends. Now, sixty years after its introduction, the Piaggio scooter is as up-to-the-minute as ever—yet retains the key characteristics of the original model. Indeed, the PX series, which flanks the recently introduced LX and Granturismo versions, still features the original 2-stroke engine, handlebar gear shift, pedal-operated brake, and spare wheel that caused such a stir back in 1946.

Much of its success has relied on inspired technical solutions, such as the sheet metal body. By providing motorized transport for the masses, the humble Vespa has helped raise living standards for at least five generations. And it looks set to continue that mission for quite some time to come. During its first years, the Vespa's main goal was to provide a balance of practicality and economy. But as time passed it was called upon to do much more. In the wake of enormous success, there would also be times of difficulty correlating with important modifications, not all of which were spot-on. Despite some failures, such as the initial attempts to apply starter engines and automatic gearboxes to the more classic models and the idea of changing the name of such a long lived product, there have also been strategies of outstanding effectiveness. One such example is the creation of a 50 cc Vespa to counter the drop in sales caused by Italy's 1962 introduction of compulsory number plates for all two-wheel vehicles over 49 cc. Another is the decision not to give in to the temptation to replace the metal bodywork with the plastic panels seen on nearly all of today's scooters.

Today's Vespa continues to fulfill its role as a cheap, practical means of transport, embracing its past while maintaining an inimitable style. Whether it's a Vespa of yesteryear or one hot off the production line, it's always a Vespa. There's no risk of confusing it with anything else! And all those features form a neat package that is compliant with the latest environmental standards while fashionable and trend-setting as ever. This book pays homage to a vehicle that is in a class of its own, a scooter that tackled— well ahead of its time—the traffic congestion that now afflicts roads the world over.

Vespa has achieved success without arrogance, attained worldwide popularity, and become one of the most long-lived products in motor vehicle history. Not one to rest on its laurels, it continues to improve to this day.

Thank you, Vespa!

11

History

Without a shadow of a doubt, the Vespa is Piaggio's most famous product. Yet it was not the only one or even the first. The origins of the brand go all the way back to 1884, in a sawmill in Sestri Ponente, near Genoa, which used to produce interior furnishings for ships. Just twenty-five years later, a steadily expanding rail network led Rinaldo Piaggio to set up a railway carriage production plant at Finale Ligure. At the beginning of the 1930s, things had expanded to include the production of high-speed, stainless steel, electrically powered railcars similar to those used in the United States. Another division involved in the production of military aircraft and seaplanes had been started following Italy's entry into the First World War in 1916. The division expanded rapidly, with the launch of many ambitious projects, and by 1923 Piaggio had become one of the biggest players in the aeronautics industry. With yet another world war looming, development focused on the needs of civil aviation and bomber production. By 1945, when the conflict was over, reconversion of the production plants was inevitable.

In 1924, Genoa-based Piaggio moved its aeronautical operations to a small automobile plant it acquired. By the end of the war in 1945, this successful division was faced with the challenge of reconversion. The Pontedera technical office, which had been transferred to Biella during the Second World War, was assigned the task of coming up with a valid concept.

15

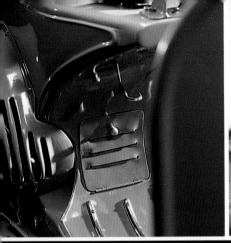

The project—to provide new solutions for the transportation sector—was headed by Corradino D'Ascanio, an aviation engineer. His task was to develop a vehicle that would be comfortable, easy to ride, and where "the engine of which cannot be seen from the outside" per Enrico Piaggio's insistence. D'Ascanio was no motorcycle fan and was thus well inclined to come up with something different.

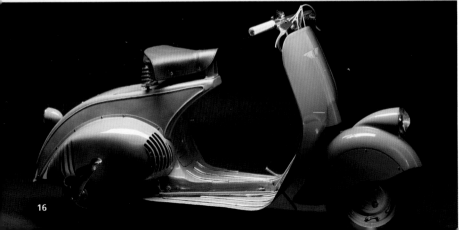

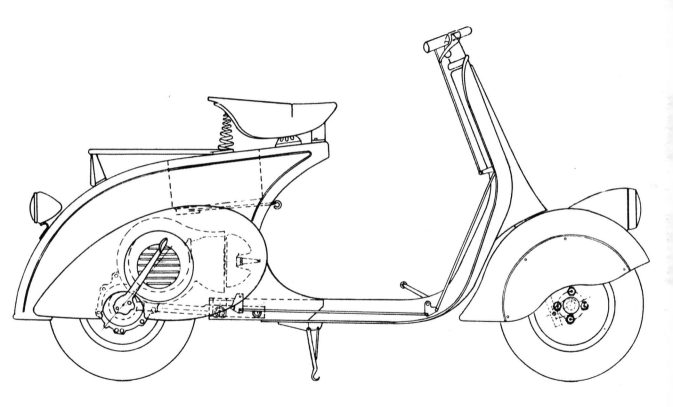

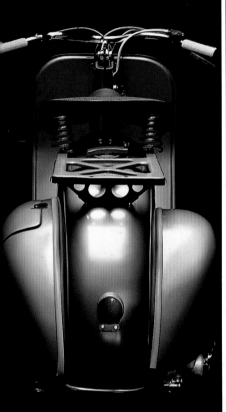

Corradino D'Ascanio had no qualms about borrowing ideas from other industries. He chose to cover the engine completely and position it out of the rider's way just as would be done with a car. The single-fork suspension was taken from aircraft design. And instead of a skeletal frame, he opted for a load-bearing sheet metal body. The project moved along quickly, and just three months later, the first prototypes were puttering out of the factory at Pontedera.

Unshackled from the traditions of the car and motorcycle industries, Piaggio came up with a truly innovative vehicle that, with the arrival of the MP6 prototype in December of 1945 (see page 16), broke the motorcycling mold forever. In April of the following year came the first mass-produced 98 cc Vespa (see page 18).

23

24

It was the first stages of the Vespa's life that saw the biggest design changes. The project was a winner, yet would require some serious tweaking to make it more practical. In 1948, the first proper suspension systems were introduced, improving stability and comfort. Between 1953 and 1955, the scooter took on the appearance that remains with us, slight modifications aside, to this day. A long seat replaced the classic saddle, and the headlight was shifted from the mudguard to the handlebars, which, in turn, were made more aerodynamic. Before long, the Vespa had become a worldwide phenomenon, as the photo depicting a Vespa rider shaking hands with Mexican President Adolfo Lopez Mateos during his visit to Buenos Aires clearly demonstrates.

This winning Italian formula was exported everywhere, from Belgium—where you could ride three to a scooter—to Turkey. From the 1950s to the 1960s, output grew exponentially. While just 2,484 Vespas were made in 1946, it was not long before the figure reached one hundred thousand. To be more precise, 131,085 Vespas were built in 1951: by 1953, half a million had been made, and in 1956, the one millionth Vespa rolled off the production line at Pontedera.

The Vespa revolutionized the very idea of what it was to be a motorcyclist and appealed as much to women as it did to men. Women were no longer just passengers riding sidesaddle (now strictly prohibited by the Italian highway code): they were up front and in control. These significant social changes were brought about by the absence of a fuel tank between seat and handlebars, thus allowing women to wear skirts and ride. Moreover, the front fairing shielded the rider's legs from bad weather, making it a practical runabout even in chilly Copenhagen.

The glamorous celebrity astride an Italian scooter is part of the collective imagery shared by all of us: the snapshots, production stills, and reels of film seem endless. Bear in mind, too, that many of these are not stunts or gimmicks, but real-life images, as the actors would often make use of their free time by buzzing around on a Vespa! These pages depict a scene from the Italian film *Il Mondo di notte*, a documentary set in the nightclubs of the world's big cities, and an emblematic photo of a young John Wayne.

One of the key features of the Vespa was the completely concealed engine beneath the rear bulges on the body. At the same time, its most traditional aspect was the horizontally mounted, single-cylinder 2-stroke engine itself, with forced-air cooling: in this respect, little has changed from the MP6 prototype to the present-day PX.

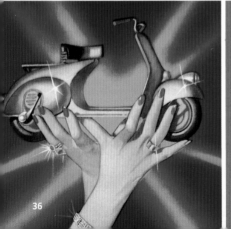

In the wake of the first 98 cc model of 1946, there followed 125, 150, 160, 180, and 200 cc versions, while the more compact models featured the 50, 90, and 125 cc engines.

LA PLUS GRANDE PRODUCTION MONDIALE

Vous

Villemot

The Vespa introduced several innovative solutions to the two-wheeled world—some as relevant now as they were then—such as the single-arm suspension. Also, the Vespa's rear-mounted engine actually pivoted on the frame and, beginning in 1948, acted as a swing-arm for anchoring the shock absorber. At the front, there is a tubular arm connected to an oscillating brake hangar and the suspension. The advantage of such a design was that it made changing the wheel a relatively simple process; though this is no longer the case with the current generation of automatic-transmission Vespas.

If only

we had...

Vespa est le scooter le plus diffusé dans le mond

Pour le tourisme

Pour le médecin

Pour les achats

Pour le sport

Like all 2-stroke engines, the Vespa's had to be refuelled from special oil-gasoline mixer pumps. Early versions required 5% oil content, but by the 1960s, the proportion of oil dropped to 2%, thanks to the introduction of rotary disc timing. In 1972, a separate mixing system made its apearance, offered as an option on the Vespa Rally.

In the decade following its launch, the Vespa reached countries that had previously been untouched by Italian exports. Vespas were soon a common sight in Hong Kong (photo, right) and even in Japan, where it was brought over by soldiers of the American Occupation force that had previously been stationed in Europe. Official importation and a proper spare parts service began in 1959.

43

Vespa "Bazooka" 1959

Back by popular demand, the modern Vespa—now fully compliant with strict American environmental standards—has reestablished itself in the United States. Half a century ago, the first wave of ground-breaking Italian scooters had proved immensely popular with Americans. Exports also made their way to Australia, where the Vespa was even used by the police force.

ECONOMY TRANSPORT
AND
LOCAL GOVERNMENT

45

Among the many successful design features were easy access to the engine and other mechanical parts and extremely simple maintenance and repair. Highly detailed handbooks provided owners with an in-depth understanding of the Vespa's workings, allowing them to undertake the most common repairs on their own. The Vespas of yesteryear also had the virtue of allowing for makeshift repairs, letting the rider continue on his way until a more permanent solution could be applied.

la **Vespa**
non dà
scosse

India soon became a strategic market for the Piaggio scooter. Advantageous economic conditions there led to the establishment of the first production lines outside the parent plant in Pontedera. In addition to the classic scooter, the Bombay factory also enjoyed considerable success with a three-wheeled variant, popularly known as the Ape, that was used as a taxi.

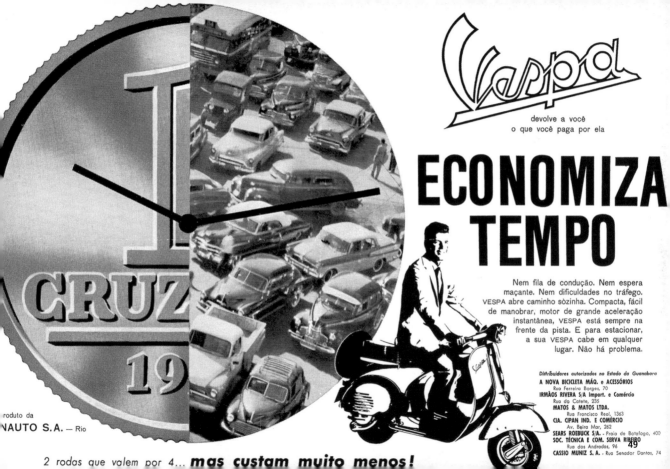

Vespa

devolve a você
o que você paga por ela

ECONOMIZA TEMPO

Nem fila de condução. Nem espera maçante. Nem dificuldades no tráfego. VESPA abre caminho sòzinha. Compacta, fácil de manobrar, motor de grande aceleração instantânea, VESPA está sempre na frente da pista. E para estacionar, a sua VESPA cabe em qualquer lugar. Não há problema.

Distribuidores autorizados no Estado da Guanabara
A NOVA BICICLETA MÁQ. e ACESSÓRIOS
Rua Ferreira Borges, 70
IRMÃOS RIVERA S/A Import. e Comércio
Rua do Catete, 235
MATOS & MATOS LTDA.
Rua Francisco Real, 1363
CIA. CIPAN IND. E COMÉRCIO
Av. Beira Mar, 262
SEARS ROEBUCK S/A. - Praia de Botafogo, 400
SOC. TÉCNICA E COM. SERVA RIBEIRO
Rua dos Andradas, 96
CASSIO MUNIZ S. A. - Rua Senador Dantas, 74

produto da
NAUTO S.A. — Rio

2 rodas que valem por 4... **mas custam muito menos!**

49

It is a little-known fact that the Vespa, a hit with famous singers and actors, resulted from the mothballing of a previous project. Prior to the MP6-Vespa, a number of prototypes of the MP5-Paperino had been built. The name (literally "Little Duck") would probably have been just as well-liked, but the scooter itself was a decidedly more conventional, slimmer affair that featured technical solutions much more in line with those on current motorcycles.

Despite having no previous experience with motorcycles, Piaggio created a vehicle that was widely appreciated for its reliability. Mechanical simplicity and structural solidity resulted in a unique product that could, without any modification, be used anywhere—from the tarmac roads of Europe to the torrid dirt tracks of Africa.

The Vespa's innovative load-bearing body proved to be a huge bonus, as it meant you could really load up! While originally conceived as a two-wheeled alternative to the economy car, the Vespa, in fact, offered two comfortable seating places. And as long as the kids stayed small, that number could be expanded to four (or even five!), and there was plenty of space on the footboard for a few bags as well. Capacity could be extended even further by attaching luggage racks.

With hundreds of thousands of scooters zipping about worldwide, it was not long before someone came up with the idea of bringing all those Vespa owners together in organized rallies. The Vespa Club d'Italia, founded in Viareggio in 1949, soon attracted more than fifty thousand members. This club—one of the biggest of its kind in the world—immediately set about organizing touring and sporting events.

Above all, an economy vehicle should provide practicality and reliability: performance is a secondary matter. Nevertheless, the early Vespa years saw rapid improvements on this front, as manufacturer-indicated top speeds clearly show. The first 98 cc version of 1946 could do 60 kph (about 37 mph), but the 125 cc, which followed just two years later, could hit 70 kph (about 44 mph). With the 150 GS of 1955 the Vespa broke the 100 kph barrier (about 63 mph).

Unlike most motorcycles, the body of the Vespa has an extensive surface area, making it ideal for customization. Before long there were numerous accessories dedicated to the Vespa, from the footboards for sidesaddle passengers to the windshield. Piaggio, along with many other manufacturers, has continued to offer a wide range of accessories.

62

The sheer popularity of the
Piaggio scooter meant that it
would inevitably be glimpsed
on the pages of the world's
newspapers. On the previous
page, it appears with a collection of products chosen by the
American magazine *Esquire* for
their outstanding design (1966).
The photo at far left shows a
Vespa at the Vatican: it was one
of the vehicles used by Enrico
Piaggio and his delegation on
the occasion of an audience
with Pope Pious XII in 1949.

Because of its unique construction, the manufacture of the Vespa adhered to methods that had more in common with automobiles than with motorcycles. The most notable process remains the transformation of sheet metal into a load-bearing body. By the 1950s, this process was already extensively automated: panels were shaped by multiple 900-ton presses, and assembly of the seats was done by electronically controlled welders.

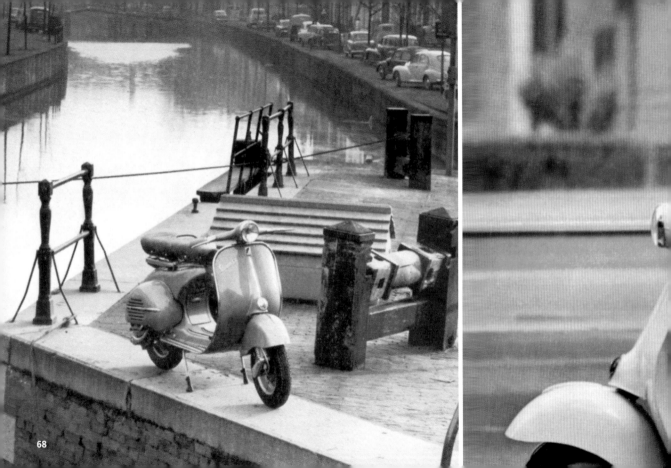

Only the absence of helmets and the position of the passenger (now strictly regulated by the Italian highway code) provide clues to a photograph's period of origin. The Vespa's design has remained virtually unchanged since its inception, undergoing improvements yet always remaining faithful to the original. Its additional role as the antidote to urban traffic congestion is as relevant now as ever.

Bigger! Better! Faster! The Vespa's single-cylinder 2-stroke engines evolved quickly in terms of size and technology. The 98 cc engines of the first series grew in 1948 to 125 cc, and in 1954 they were enlarged again to 150 cc. The 200 cc models arrived in 1972.

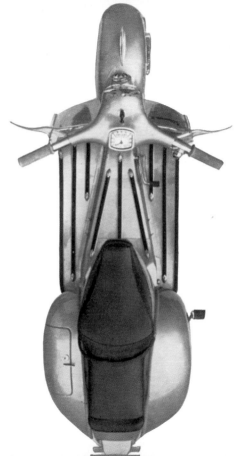

In 1962, there came a need to extend the product range "downwards" after a modification to the Italian highway code that allowed anyone over the age of fourteen to ride models of up to 49 cc without a license. A year later what would soon be known as the "Vespino" was born. In 1965 the Vespa 50 classic evolved into the SS90, a model with a narrower front fairing, a specially designed exhaust, and a spare wheel and storage compartment between seat and footboard. In 1968 came the 125 Primavera, the largest of the "Vespini."

In 1977, the Vespa Nuova Linea made its debut, characterized by the PX symbol, produced with 125 and 200 cc engines and joined a year later by a 150 cc model. Although still quite big, its sharper, slimmer, and less rounded appearance sparked renewed interest in the Vespa. Despite attempts to have it replaced altogether, popular demand has obliged Piaggio to continue its production. The PX has recently been restyled, sporting new instrumentation, a vintage Vespa logo (instead of the one from 1970s), a front disc brake, and even a catalytic converter to comply with antipollution laws.

In 1982 there was the launch of the new compact series. It included the classic 50 and the PK, which replaced the earlier Special, with its squared headlight and handlebars, and the 125 Primavera, which had identical engine displacements. Despite modern lines and more sophisticated technical features, such as a front suspension borrowed from the PX, sales were sluggish. Automatic transmissions were first introduced with this series.

To celebrate its first half-century in 1996, the Vespa underwent radical changes, evident in the new ET series, sold alongside the PX. Between the two there was a clear generation gap, yet they still shared the ideas that counted, such as the pressed metal bodywork. The engines were shifted from their traditional right-hand position and were all new, the 125 version being upgraded to 4-stroke and its handlebar gears replaced in favor of an automatic transmission. The first 50 cc 2-stroke injection model was also introduced.

With the introduction of the ET series came the need for a modernized large version of the Vespa. This gap was filled in 2003 by the launch of the Vespa Granturismo. While featuring the by now indispensable load-bearing metal body, it nevertheless established a number of firsts: it was the biggest Vespa ever, the first to mount 12-inch diameter wheels as opposed to the traditional 10 inches, and also featured disc brakes. Liquid-cooled, 4-valve, 4-stroke 125 and 200 cc engines completed the package.

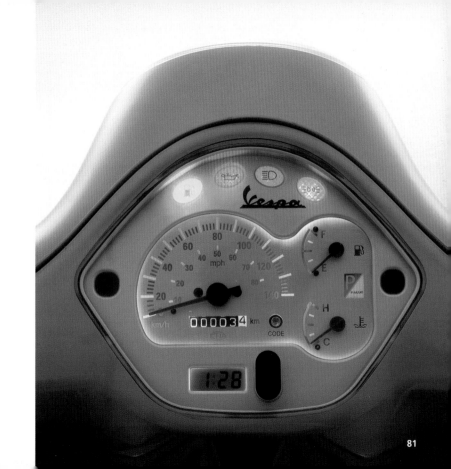

In 2005 the LX replaced the ET: in just nine years some 480,000 of the latter had been sold, raising the number of Vespas scattered across the world to a staggering 16 million. In addition to aesthetic modifications, important technical changes were also made to the Vespino. The classic 10-inch wheels were replaced with 11-inch wheels, and a choice of four engines became available: 50 cc 2 stroke and 50, 125, and 150 cc 4 stroke.

At press time, the very latest model (the 140th since 1946) is the GTS 250 i.e. Based on the Granturismo and built to celebrate the fiftieth anniversary of the launch of the original GS, it is officially the most powerful and fastest Vespa ever. The 250 cc, liquid-cooled, 4-valve engine packs 22 hp, allowing it to reach a top speed of 122 kph (about 76 mph).

It may well have the most powerful and fastest configuration of them all, but the Vespa GTS, like the original model, remains a sound, economic alternative to the automobile. There are also numerous useful extras: some are classic, such as the front and rear luggage racks and footboard mat, while others, such as the novel all-weather cover that attaches magnetically to the body, are much more recent. The GTS also has another important option: an antilock braking system (ABS).

The scooters shown at left are divided by sixty years of history. Throughout that time, the Vespa has evolved successfully while remaining faithful to its original design concept. Today's style draws on that of yesteryear—and the only characteristics that have fallen by the wayside are those rendered obsolete by new safety or emissions-control legislation. Less evident are the numerous developments that have been made on the manufacturing side, where Piaggio has maintained a tradition of cutting-edge production systems for its scooter.

Competitions and records

The world on two wheels is a tad competitive by nature, and motorcyclists will attempt to race anything, no matter how innocuous it might look. If the access roads of the Monza race circuit were willing to host endurance competitions for Velosolexes, then the amount of sporting activity generated by the Vespa in its sixty-year career is easily guessed at. Whether official, unofficial, serious, or silly, the number of organized events was—and is—endless. The Vespa has been a protagonist of major events, ranging from official participation and outstanding success in the off-road Sei Giorni di Regolarità to numerous attempts at world speed and endurance records, some of which still stand.

Vespas were transformed to allow participation in endurance and even trial competitions, an area usually reserved for the off-road daredevils. Trial events were all the rage in the 1970s, the most important being the twenty-four hour race in Montjuich, a sort of Bol d'Or for scooters on an inner-city circuit of Barcelona. Alongside the more serious events, controlled by the Motorcycling Federation, there was—and still is—no shortage of impromptu competitions, which, without the Vespa, would probably never have taken place.

Motorcycle-paced races are just one of many types of indoor cycling events: the Vespa looks quite at home high up on the raised bends, especially when setting the pace for road champions of the caliber of Anquetil and Coppi. The other two photos on this page have more of a novelty appeal: the scooters here are being used as harness racing "horses" to tow their carriages in an impromptu event. Even odder is the picture of a Vespa involved in a bull-fight: the photo, as might be expected, was taken in Madrid, Spain.

93

The record-breaking fever that gripped just about every motor vehicle manufacturer of the 1950s was inevitably caught by Piaggio. The euphoria of the moment and the intense rivalry with Innocenti, the Milan-based manufacturer of the Lambretta, drove the technicians at Pontedera to make repeated attempts at several world records: an activity in which the Pontedera plant was able to employ all the aerodynamic knowledge it had acquired during its aircraft-making days. At Monthléry in 1950, a Vespa with a streamlined fairing and tail fin smashed seventeen world records in just ten hours. The following year, at Ostia, a beautiful torpedolike 125 cc established a new flying kilometer record of 171.102 kph (about 106 mph).

In 1955, with the arrival of the Vespa GS, more people became "sports" enthusiasts. Scooters soon started trying out their newfound power against conventional motor-cycles in on-road competitions. Events such as the Giro Vespistico dei Tre Mari (right) from Campania to Sicily and the Cimento Invernale, held in Lombardy, appeared. Off-road successes were also plentiful, such as the triumph in the Sei Giorni di Regolarità of 1951, in which the Vespas were outfitted with two spare wheels and an enlarged fuel tank.

98

One of the toughest races in which the Piaggio scooter competed was undoubtedly the Paris-Dakar of 1980. French riders Simonot and Tcherniawsky chose a PX 200, modifying the rear section to obtain the autonomy required by the rule book. Despite the magnitude of the challenge, they made it all the way to the finish line on the shores of Senegal. They were assisted by a route that, in this second edition of the race, was somewhat smoother than the one taken today; it did not include high sand dunes. Yet the result was historical nonetheless, as it remains the only time the race has been completed by riders on nonendurance motorcycles.

A taste for adventure

The Vespa is not just the holder of the scooter world's longevity record. Despite its docile, congenial appearance, it has provided inspiration for adventurous voyages that have at times verged on the impossible and feats that merit a place in the Guinness book of records. Many of these journeys were done purely for the sake of spending endless hours on a Vespa or the sheer fun of completing an unconventional challenge. The majority of these accomplishments are concentrated in the early Vespa years, during a period in which records of every kind were being broken. These were also the years in which the Piaggio motorcycling team offered up its precision riding displays. Rather than

being a drawback, having smaller wheels and a smaller engine than most other two-wheeled vehicles provided added stimulus to do things out of the ordinary and put the Vespa in the history books. Parallel trends are seen in other fields, especially the automobile industry, where the most adventurous journeys were, in fact, completed in Volkswagen Beetles, Citroen 2CVs, and Renault 4s, the four-wheeled equivalents of the Italian scooter. Thanks to this taste for adventure, the collective distance covered by the 16 million Vespas scattered across the world is unimaginable; although we are certainly talking about billions of miles.

The claim that the Vespa has conquered every continent is not an idle one. In 1963, for example, Soren Nielsen rode one to the polar ice shelf. The following year an Italian journalist named Roberto Patrignani covered the eight thousand miles that separate Milan from Tokyo on a Vespa 150, specially outfitted to cope with the rigors of the journey. In addition to the custom luggage racks, it featured an auxiliary 17-liter fuel tank placed directly behind the leg guard.

Georges Monneret's journey smacks of the incredible. After leaving Paris at midnight on October 8, 1952, he rode to Calais, where he mounted his Vespa on a specially made raft and then "rode" twenty miles to Dover, England. Despite some mechanical hitches and rough seas, he managed to cross the channel in five and a half hours. Upon reaching the English coast, he continued on to London, thus becoming the first person in the world to make the trip without changing vehicles. The Alpha Vespa, however, never existed: it was just a mock-up used for the 1967 spy film, *Dick Smart*.

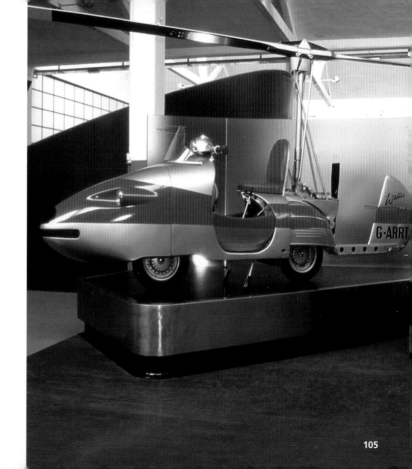

Among the Vespa's many endurance feats is one completed by the author. To support the launch of a book on the Italian scooter, he organized a twenty-four-hour nonstop ride on a standard Vespa Special 50 on December 3 and 4, 1979. The goal was to cover six hundred miles, the maximum distance that, according to the 25 mph speed limit of the time, a scooter would travel in one day.

24 hours on a Vespa

Quasi 1000 km in una 24 ore «non stop» alla guida di una Vespa 50 cmc Special

Si è concluso positivamente l'esperimento tentato da un giovane studente milanese. Valerio Boni, 20 anni, è riuscito a guidare una Vespa 50 special per 24 ore consecutive senza mai arrestarsi. L'esperimento organizzato dalla rivista Tuttovespa in collaborazione con la Piaggio, ha avuto luogo sabato e domenica sulla pista Pirelli di Vizzola Ticino. Boni è partito alle 20 di sabato (starter è stato Virginio Ferrari), ma dopo più di un'ora e mezzo si è dovuto arrestare per un problema alla candela. E' ripartito quindi da zero alle 22,18 concludendo la sua fatica esattamente dopo 24 ore, domenica sera. Questo il risultato: 420 giri e mezzo della pista che misura 2235 metri; la distanza percorsa è stata di 940 km. 118 metri e 69 centimetri. Più o meno la stessa distanza che intercorre fra Milano e Parigi. La prestazione è curiosa se si pensa che il conduttore non si è mai arrestato, nemmeno per fare rifornimento (eseguito in movimento da bordo di una Vespa 200). Valerio Boni, oltre che contro la fatica, ha dovuto lottare anche contro il freddo intenso (nella mattinata di domenica il termometro era sceso sotto lo zero) che rischiava di creare problemi tecnici (la condensa di umidità attorno al carburatore ad un certo punto si è gelata). La prova, per di più, è stata ostacolata dalla fitta nebbia che ha reso problematica la marcia nelle ultime ore.

Carefully documented by the time-keepers of the Federazione Nazionale, the test was carried out on the Pirelli track at Vizzola Ticino. The only modification with respect to the standard model was the triangular saddle instead of the standard oblong version, so as to make refuelling easier. Because the "nonstop" rules prohibited any actual stops, refuelling was done by bringing a Vespa PX 200 alongside the 50 Special on the track's longest straightaway and transferring the gasoline from a jerrycan; a rudimentary pressure pump was used to speed things up. Mechanical problems caused by damp, dense fog and cold forced a second start ninety minutes after the official one. These problems raised their heads again during the final stages of the test, lowering average speed and preventing the team from reaching their target of six hundred miles. In 420 laps the Vespa covered 585 miles, 387 feet and 27 inches.

After clocking 157,000 miles and travelling through just about every country in the world, Giorgio Bettinelli is without doubt, the king of the Vespa travellers. With his trusty Vespa PX, he has made four astounding solo journeys: Rome to Saigon (15,000 miles, seven months from 1992 to 1993, ten countries); Alaska to Tierra del Fuego (22,400 miles, nine months from 1994 to 1995, eighteen countries); Melbourne to Capetown (32,000 miles, twelve months from 1995 to 1996, twenty-three countries); Tierra del Fuego to Tasmania (89,000 miles, three years and eight months from 1997 to 2001, ninety countries).

Variations, imitations, and competitors

With any successful product, it's only a matter of time before others attempt to imitate or attack it. Imitations and competitors of the Vespa appeared everywhere, especially outside Italy, so the Vespa had a fight on its hands nearly all the time. For the first thirty years, the most dangerous rival was a "fellow Italian." In many a year, in fact, scooter sales were characterized by a neck-and-neck battle between Piaggio's Pontedera-built Vespa and the Lambretta, though there were significant design differences. Over

the years, Piaggio has developed several variations on the Vespa theme, although not every project has enjoyed the success of the scooter. For example, the three-wheeled van (initially produced with a front end almost identical to the Vespa's), economical and maneuverable even in the narrowest streets, was a clear winner, while the idea of moving into the marine engine market was far less so. The Piaggio Group has tried on several occasions over the years to come up with a successor to the Vespa, and not always successfully.

Ape!
Ape!
Ape!

Just two years after the Vespa's debut came the Ape (the Italian word for "bee," pronounced *aa-pay*). The first version of this little van had a narrow front end that was all scooter, a wider rear with two wheels, and a small truck bed. Before long, the Ape had revolutionized the light transport industry, and not just in Italy. Later on, the front end was modified to provide a proper cab, while numerous versions of the rear end offered a range of functions, public transport included. These mini people-carriers are a common sight in India and on the Isle of Capri. In the 1990s, the four-wheeled Poker version was launched, yet the three-wheeler classic remains the favorite.

Moscone

Vespa and Ape ("Wasp" and "Bee") were not the only insects to exit the Pontedera factory. Encouraged by the success of its two- and three-wheel vehicles, in 1949 Piaggio launched the Moscone (Bluebottle). This outboard engine took its stylistic and technical inspiration from one of the most successful American models of the day. Two series followed the first model, launched in 1953 and 1960 respectively. The last one had a displacement of 99.5 cc and a power rating of 3.3 hp. Despite the low price of 118,000 liras, it never managed to assert itself over the better-established rivals.

Vespa's archenemies in Europe were two very different scooters. The Lambretta became the Vespa's main rival very early on: the first prototypes appeared in 1944, and mass production at the Milan-based Innocenti plant started in October 1947. In 1971, production in Italy ended, but continued in India and Spain. In the 1980s, the French company Peugeot's Metropolis encroached on the Vespa monopoly with a whole new scooter concept: automatic gearboxes and plastic paneling.

In 1949 Piaggio issued a notice warning that anyone making, selling, or buying any of the numerous imitations of the Vespa would be prosecuted according to Italian laws on unfair competition. One such product—a blatant copy of the Vespa—was made in the Soviet Union. In 1957, after their successful cloning of the 2-cylinder BMWs left behind by the retreating Germany army at the end of the Second World War, the Russians came up with a scooter that was nearly identical to the Vespa GS. It was called the Viatka.

Before finding a viable strategy for the twenty-first century with the ET, LX, and Granturismo series, the Piaggio Group tried, several times, to come up with an alternative to its most famous scooter. One of the most notable projects was proposed under the Gilera brand name: in 1982 the GSA, an angular 50 cc model with a newly designed engine and automatic gearbox was launched. To start it, the rider would engage the transmission by rotating a grip on the handlebars; there was no clutch. In 1987 came the Cosa, which featured Vespa-like styling and mechanics under a different name. It never seriously rivalled the Vespa, not even when ABS braking and a catalytic converter were added.

Bajaj scooters officially arrived in Europe in the mid-1980s. Sales performance was good, largely thanks to two factors: low price and looks that evoked the most classic Vespas. Yet this was no brazen imitation. The Chetak, in fact, was made in India under Piaggio license by Bajaj, which, when the partnership between the two companies ended, continued production. In the wake of the first versions, which featured separate seats and rounded lines, came models that were more modern but had much less vintage charm.

The Vespa 400 / The Vespa Car

In the 1950s, Piaggio decided to follow the lead of other motorcycle manufacturers—such as BMW, NSU, DKW, and Maico—and produce its own small car. A name had already been chosen for this new vehicle—the Vespa 400—and it was to be built by the Paris-based L'Atelier de Costruction Moto et Accessoires, which was already making Vespa scooters for Piaggio at the rate of 260 per day. A preliminary design of the Vespa 400 was a direct offshoot of the scooter. The father of the Vespa, Corradino D'Ascanio, was initially put in charge of the development program; numerous options were

assessed, including that of a car with a front mounted engine and front-wheel drive, a concept that was twenty years ahead of its time. In the end, though, Piaggio opted for the "all rear" layout that was the order of the day. The design was a good one, and the Vespa 400 looked set to conquer the world; yet somehow it never managed to repeat the success of the scooter. From 1958 until the end of production in 1961, Piaggio produced just thirty-six thousand of them. The reason the Vespa 400 was quashed so soon remains a mystery.

Toward the end of the 1950s, odd never-before-seen cars began appearing on Italian roads, especially in Tuscany. While no one knew where they had come from, they did seem to confirm rumors about the imminent launch of a new Italian economy car. Production, in fact, was already under way, but not at Pontedera.

The launch of the Vespa showed that Piaggio could successfully transfer its skills beyond the confines of the ship-fitting and aeronautical areas. However, the management knew all too well that sooner or later, Vespa buyers would want to own an automobile. What was needed was a small car that could carry at least two adults and two children and offer the low cost of ownership of the famed scooter.

Bientôt...
on ne pourra plus circuler!

Paris et nos grandes villes sont de plus en plus embouteillées. Seule la VESPA 400, nerveuse et maniable, permet de se faufiler et de stationner. Elle est sans conteste le premier remède à la crise de la circulation et c'est en même temps une vraie routière. Grâce à elle : temps gagné... peine évitée... tranquillité d'esprit

la seule solution...

321.075ᶠ

LA MOINS CHÈRE

DES VOITURES

FRANÇAISES

★

131

Piaggio was certainly not the only motorcycle manufacturer of the period with plans for car production. Several German companies already had very similar ideas. As Piaggio went ahead with prelaunch testing, no one harbored any doubts about the name of the new microcar: it would be called the Vespa 400.

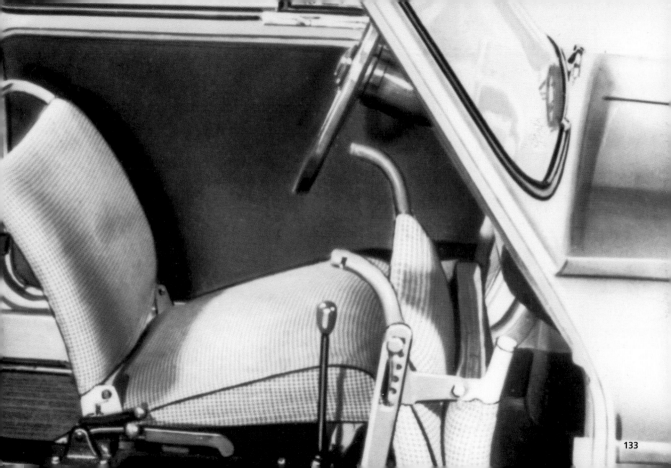

Although designed and developed in Italy, manufacturing was done at the ACMA production plants in Fourchambault, France. Based in Paris, the Atelier de Costruction Moto et Accessoires employed 2,300 workers and was already producing, under license, 260 scooters a day for Piaggio in the 123, 147, and 173 cc versions. Cars road-tested in Tuscany thus sported two license plates: the official French plate and the Italian test one.

Vespa 400

1958

DES MOYENNES ÉLEVÉES ET LE KILOMÈTRE MOINS CHE

SOUPLESSE, SILENCE, SÉCURITÉ

...ndres en ligne inclinée à 20° - 2 temps à distribution
...gée - Alésage et course 63 × 63 - Cylindrée totale
... compression 6,4 - Refroidissement par air forcé avec
... Avance automatique à l'allumage - Épurateur d'air à
... d'huile.

**ACCESSIBILITÉ TOTALE
AU MOTEUR.** La simpli-
cité du moteur est remar-
quable et son accessibilité
est totale.

Le réservoir de carburant,
d'une capacité de 23 litres

136

COTES : Voie avant : **1,10 m**
Empattement : **1,693 m** - Poids
hors tout : **1,27 m** - Longueur

On the eve of the Paris show of 1957, the Vespa 400 was put through its paces on the roads of Monte Carlo, famed for its Formula 1 race. The Argentine Juan Manuel Fangio, five-time world champion, was there. A representative for Vespa in Argentina, Fangio described the Vespa 400 as "fantastic and amazing." At the end of the test drive he said he felt as if he had been driving "a much bigger-engined car."

French drivers took an immediate liking to the little car and flocked to the Paris show to get a closer look at it. The Vespa 400 thus became the star of the event, and before long, ACMA had gathered some twenty thousand advance orders. It promised to be a car for anyone and everyone, from the wealthy person in need of a stylish runabout to the small family in search of a thrifty means of transport. Compact, with outstanding engine performance and maneuverability, it promised to resolve traffic problems in Paris and other big cities, yet was also suitable for long-distance journeys.

The Vespa 400 was powered by a 2 cylinder, 2-stroke, air-cooled 394 cc engine that produced 14 hp at 4350 rpm. Top speed was almost 56 mph, and it featured a 3-speed gearbox (plus reverse gear). In 1990, there was further talk of a Piaggio economy car. An unnamed four-wheel prototype was presented at the Cologne Car Show: it featured double rear wheels, a 280 cc, 20 hp engine with an automatic transmission, and a top speed of 60 mph.

VOITURE DE GRANDE CLASSE

Vespa 400

141

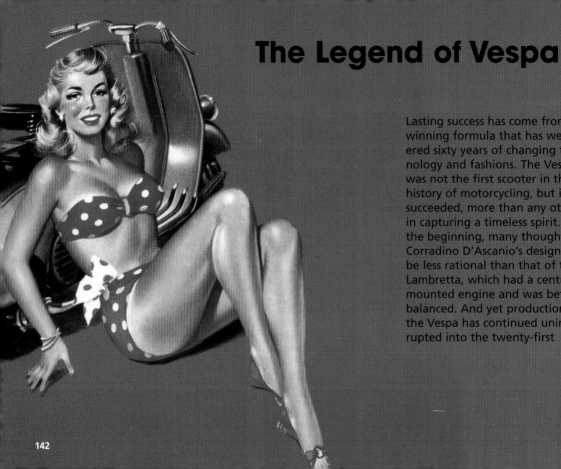

The Legend of Vespa

Lasting success has come from a winning formula that has weathered sixty years of changing technology and fashions. The Vespa was not the first scooter in the history of motorcycling, but it succeeded, more than any other, in capturing a timeless spirit. In the beginning, many thought Corradino D'Ascanio's design to be less rational than that of the Lambretta, which had a centrally mounted engine and was better balanced. And yet production of the Vespa has continued uninterrupted into the twenty-first

century. Such longevity is shared by only a very few, such as the Harley Davidson motorcycles, the Volkswagen Beetle, and the Mini. Piaggio's scooter has withstood the test of time, becoming an icon for generations of people thanks to unforgettable advertising campaigns and unmistakable lines that no competitor has ever been able to better. The Vespa is a rare product that has swum against the tide of fashion and succeeded in setting the trend for generations of two-wheel vehicle users.

948-86

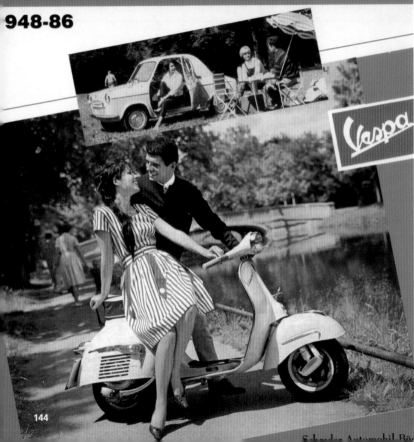

Vespa

Schrader Automobil-Ba

The Vespa is one of the products that made the rest of the world stand up and take notice of Italy. It soon become a common sight all over the world. Outstandingly practical, it had the good luck to become a status symbol. Not immediately affordable to all, the Vespa was first purchasable by installment through Sarpi, the financial division specially created by Piaggio for this purpose and one of the first companies of its kind in Italy.

Vespa G.S.

paradiso per due

Vespa

a paradise for two

145

Vespa

Elégance

Sécurité

Confort

Economie

ils sont heureux...

Vive le printemps...

IN VESPA DA MILANO A TOKYO

In Italy, as in the rest of Europe and the world, the Piaggio scooter soon outgrew its role as a cheap alternative to the car. It came to symbolize freedom, coolness, and comfort and quickly proved its worth as a vehicle for medium and long-distance trips. Others saw the Vespa as something more than this, as its success on numerous adventure journeys clearly demonstrated.

147

In the 1950s and the 1960s, the Vespa was all the rage. No one, from ordinary workers to film stars and sports celebrities, could resist the temptation to be photographed next to the world's coolest scooter. Vespas appeared in numerous films, playing a "starring" role in features such as *Roman Holiday* and *La Dolce Vita* and a supporting one on the posters for *Mia Nonna Poliziotto* with Tina Pica.

al posto
di lavoro?

Vespizzatevi

•149

Traffic in the post-Second World War days was certainly not as congested as it is now. Nevertheless, the importance of a vehicle that was slimmer and lighter than a car was not lost on the advertising companies. In addition to promoting the concept of evolution, advertisements also touted the Vespa as a valid alternative to owning a "four-wheeled sardine can."

At the time of Carosello (an advertising slot on Italian television in the 1950s and 1960s), when ad messages were simple and direct, Piaggio launched a classic campaign: the slogan "chi Vespa mangia le mele (chi non Vespa no)" proved to be near-unforgettable. Loosely translated as "those who Vespa, eat apples (those who don't Vespa, don't)," it featured an image of the classic forbidden fruit with two nibbles taken out of the sides. This effective ad, devised by Gilberto Filippetti, ran from 1968 to 1971.

Vespa
The Nobility of Mobility

KING OF SPEED
The Vespa 150 c.c. Gran Sport. £188.8.3 incl. P.T.

LORD OF ELEGANCE
The Vespa 150 c.c. £160,10,2 incl. P.T.

PRINCE OF PERFECTION
The Vespa 125 c.c. 125 Gns. incl. P.T.

ACCESSORIES IN WAITING
See the bright new range at your Dealer now.

Betta Getta Vespa

The World's Finest Scooter with the 12-month Guarantee
Douglas (Sales & Service) Ltd., Kingswood, Bristol
Division of Westinghouse Brake and Signal Co. Ltd.

Un giorno un piccolo aereo lasciò le ali in cielo per diventare un mito in terra.

Era il giorno
di una intuizione perfetta, fatta per durare.
Era una idea circondata da piccole, misteriose
leggende, che la volevano figlia dell'aria,
scesa dal cielo per correre leggera,
sicura della sua nobile origine aeronautica.
Così Vespa abbandonò le ali per vestirsi di una
forma d'acciaio diventata grande nei nostri cuori.
Vespa figlia dell'aria.

Vespa, il mito scooter.

PIAGGIO

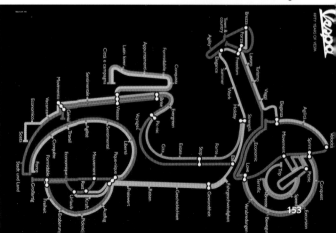

153

IO VESPA, TU JANE

VESPA, LA TUA LIANA IN CITTÀ

la tua Vespa
chiedila agli
UOMINI AZZURRI

L'HANNO VISTA TUTTI

IO NE HO PARLATO A LUNGO

PER ME HA FATTO MODA

PER ME HA SUPERATO TUTTI

chi Vespa

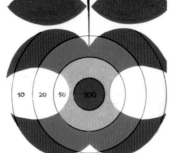

MI HA SORPRESO MOLTO

PER ME HA FATTO CENTRO

10 20 50 100

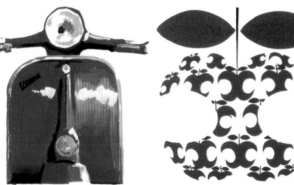

LA VESPA NATURALMENTE

CHE SUCCESSO RAGAZZI

mangia le mele

Oggi sono la vetta.

vespa

PIAGGIO

Når De har bestemt Dem for Vespa - så har De
samtidig bestemt Dem for god og velorganiseret service.
Overalt her i landet - ja, overalt i verden - findes
et net af autoriserede Vespa servicestationer, hvor De altid vil
blive betjent af folk, der kender Deres køretøj ud og ind.
De vil overalt kunne få originale reservedele til fornuftige priser.

De har også bestemt Dem for det mærke, der som brugt
køretøj vurderes til højere priser end andre mærker. Det vil få
betydning for Dem den dag, De skal sælge eller bytte.
De har valgt rigtigt, når De nu vælger Vespa.

IMPORT: F. BÜLOW & CO. KBHVN.

BERGENHOLZ & ARNESEN
VANG RASMUSSEN

156

Long before the 1996 set of posters celebrating fifty years of the Vespa appeared—signed by renowned artists such as Milton Glaser, Shigeo Fukuda, and Italo Lupi (see page 153)—the Italian scooter had been the subject of many an artist and illustrator, each of whom high-lighted a different aspect, such as the styling or the practicality of the spare wheel. Images of the insect from which it takes its name (the wasp) are surpris-ingly rare.

at play with THE PLAYMATES

158

The Vespa's appearances outside its natural habitat of the highway were not limited to advertising and film: pictures of the Vespa abounded on vinyl record sleeves, too. Two non-Italian examples are seen on records by Don Elliott and the Playmates.

The Italian scooter remains a protagonist even in the era of CD and MP3. In 1999, the popular Italian band Lunapop had a hit single with "Vespa Special," a song about a 1970's model that was extremely popular with young people. On the eve of the new millennium, the song extended the Vespa's fame even further, despite the technological divide, which by then separated it from modern plastic-shelled scooters.

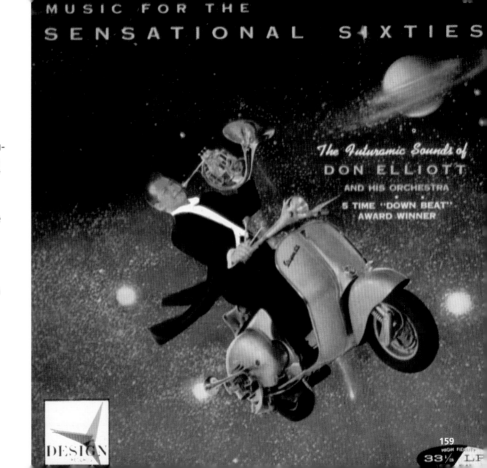

In addition to the "in-house" advertising, there was no shortage of ad campaigns in which suppliers boasted of their partnership with Piaggio (such as Pirelli in 1979). In other cases, especially during the first few years of its production, the Vespa was publicized using rather direct messages. Most notably, between 1957 and 1959, Piaggio focused on facts and figures, such as exports breaking the fifty thousand barrier, or a 62 percent share of total sales on the Italian market. In 1949, a more aggressive "beware of imitations" approach was taken to counteract Vespa's rivals.

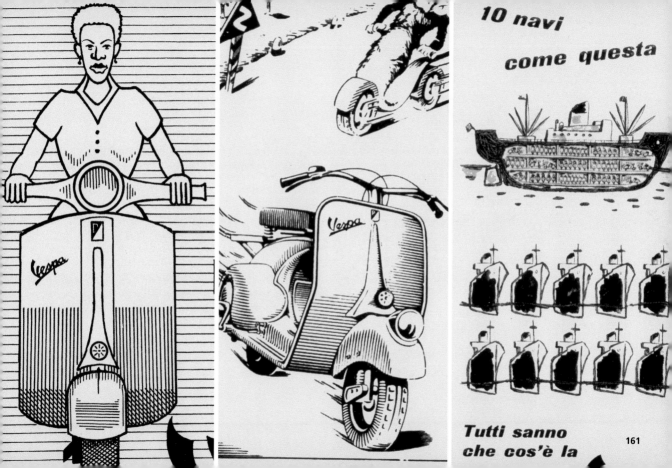

10 navi

come questa

Tutti sanno
che cos'è la

Depicted in many an entertaining combination with animals and objects, the Vespa also proved to be a perfect match for the pinup girl of the 1950s. Renowned examples were the calendars that ran from 1951 to 1954: featuring the unmistakable artwork of Franco Mosca, they are now valuable collectors' items. In 1955, hand-drawn beauties were replaced by real ones. First came the models with the classic, busty lines of Italian beauties. From 1962 they were followed by a long line of stars that included Gina Lollobrigida and Ursula Andress.

lo scooter
più venduto nel mondo

Vespa

Scansati baloccone

Per VESPA 50 lo stile non è solo un fatto estetico, non è un optional.
È il frutto di un design razionale, il punto di arrivo di una evoluzione che solo una grande azienda come

Piaggio può permettersi.
VESPA 50 si differenzia da tutto e da tutti per tre caratteristiche che la rendono unica:
□ le marce, per una guida in grado di dare sempre

una interpretazione personale della strada
□ la carrozzeria autoportante, stampata in un solo blocco, che porta con sè un concetto rivoluzionario per il mondo del due ruote

□ l'acciaio con cui è costruita, certezza di solidità e sicurezza di guida in ogni circostanza
Perché VESPA 50 è un mito che resta.

164

vespa 50 **gelosia d'acciaio con tre marce**

 PIAGGIO

When the Vespa was originaly launched, it was essential to transmit a message that would tell the public just what the two-wheeled Piaggio was capable of. By later years the message required modification. In the 1980s, for example, advertisements emphasized the advantages of the all-metal body to counter the competition from the new plastic-shelled scooters (the campaign was again managed by Gilberto Filipetti).

per il vostro lavoro
per il vostro svago

Vespizzatevi

Vespa in the comics

A vehicle as legendary as the Vespa inevitably would be featured in the world of comic books. It has made countless appearances in comics for readers of every age. Scooters with the classic Piaggio lines have regularly appeared in popular Italian comics such as *Topolino* and *Diabolik*. In the 1970s, a Vespa was the inseparable companion of a tough looking stuntman in *Il Giornalino*, published by Edizioni Paoline. One of the biggest advocates of the Vespa was undoubtedly Benito Jacovitti, creator of Coccobill and other popular characters such as Pasqualino. The silhouette of a vintage Vespa scooter appears regularly in his stories.

CINQUANT'ANNI DELLA "VESPA"

Vespa

ITALIA 750

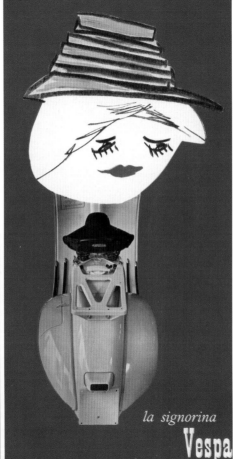

la signorina **Vespa**

On April 28, 1956—just ten years after it creation—the one millionth Vespa rolled off the production line at Pontedera. Success of such magnitude had not been achieved anywhere else in the two-wheeled world. To honor the event, a special seal was used by Piaggio in all of its correspondence. The Italian Post Office issued a commemorative stamp in June of the same year.

168

169

Technical notes

This section provides images and key specifications on Vespa models that introduced new features. A listing of all versions sold on the Italian market from 1946 to the present day follows.

1 98

Model Year: 1946
Engine: 98 cc, 2 stroke
Transmission: 3 speed
Power: 3 hp
Top Speed: 37 mph
Weight: 132 lbs
Wheel Size: 3.50 x 8"

2 125 elastico

Model Year: 1948
Engine: 124.8 cc, 2 stroke
Transmission: 3 speed
Power: 4 hp
Top Speed: 43 mph
Weight: 154 lbs
Wheel Size: 3.50 x 8"

3 125 cambio flessibile

Model Year: 1951
Engine: 124.8 cc, 2 stroke
Transmission: 3 speed
Power: 4 hp
Top Speed: 43 mph
Weight: 187 lbs
Wheel Size: 3.50 x 8"

4 125 mod 53U

Model Year: 1953
Engine: 123.5 cc, 2 stroke
Transmission: 3 speed
Power: 4.5 hp
Top Speed: 40 mph
Weight: 172 lbs
Wheel Size: 3.50 x 8"

5 150 GS

Model Year: 1955
Engine: 145.6 cc, 2 stroke
Transmission: 4 speed
Power: 8 hp
Top Speed: 63 mph
Weight: 244 lbs
Wheel Size: 3.50 x 10"

6 150

Model Year: 1957
Engine: 145.6 cc, 2 stroke
Transmission: 3 speed
Power: 5.4 hp
Top Speed: 52 mph
Weight: 216 lbs
Wheel Size: 3.50 x 8"

7 125

Model Year: 1959
Engine: 123.4 cc, 2 stroke
Transmission: 3 speed
Power: 4.6 hp
Top Speed: 49 mph
Weight: 202 lbs
Wheel Size: 3.50 x 8"

8 160 GS

Model Year: 1962
Engine: 158.5 cc, 2 stroke
Transmission: 4 speed
Power: 8.9 hp
Top Speed: 63 mph
Weight: 244 lbs
Wheel Size: 3.50 x 10"

9 50

Model Year: 1963
Engine: 49.8 cc, 2 stroke
Transmission: 3 speed
Power: 1.4 hp
Top Speed: 25 mph
Weight: 155 lbs
Wheel Size: 2.75 x 9"

10 90

Model Year: 1963
Engine: 88.5 cc, 2 stroke
Transmission: 3 speed
Power: 3.6 hp
Top Speed: 43 mph
Weight: 164 lbs
Wheel Size: 3.00 x 10"

11 90 SS

Model Year: 1965
Engine: 88.5 cc, 2 stroke
Transmission: 4 speed
Power: 5.9 hp
Top Speed: 59 mph
Weight: 177 lbs
Wheel Size: 3.00 x 10"

12 125 Primavera

Model Year: 1968
Engine: 121.1 cc, 2 stroke
Transmission: 4 speed
Power: 5.5 hp
Top Speed: 53 mph
Weight: 172 lbs
Wheel Size: 3.00 x 10"

13 180 Rally

Model Year: 1968
Engine: 180.7 cc, 2 stroke
Transmission: 4 speed
Power: 10.3 hp
Top Speed: 65 mph
Weight: 235 lbs
Wheel Size: 3.50 x 10"

14 50 Elestart

Model Year: 1969
Engine: 49 cc, 2 stroke
Transmission: 3 speed
Power: 1.4 hp
Top Speed: 25 mph
Weight: 165 lbs
Wheel Size: 3.00 x 10"

15 50 Special

Model Year: 1969
Engine: 49 cc, 2 stroke
Transmission: 3 speed
Power: 1.4 hp
Top Speed: 25 mph
Weight: 157 lbs
Wheel Size: 3.00 x 10"

16 200 Rally

Model Year: 1972
Engine: 197.9 cc, 2 stroke
Transmission: 4 speed
Power: 12.3 hp
Top Speed: 72 mph
Weight: 237 lbs
Wheel Size: 3.50 x 10"

17 125 Primavera ET3

Model Year: 1976
Engine: 121.1 cc, 2 stroke
Transmission: 4 speed
Power: 7 hp
Top Speed: 53 mph
Weight: 172 lbs
Wheel Size: 3.00 x 10"

18 50 Special 4 marce

Model Year: 1977
Engine: 49.7 cc, 2 stroke
Transmission: 4 speed
Power: 1.5 hp
Top Speed: 25 mph
Weight: 157 lbs
Wheel Size: 3.00 x 10"

19 P125 X

Model Year: 1977
Engine: 123.4 cc, 2 stroke
Transmission: 4 speed
Power: 8 hp
Top Speed: 53 mph
Weight: 229 lbs
Wheel Size: 3.50 x 10"

20 P200 E

Model Year: 1977
Engine: 197.9 cc, 2 stroke
Transmission: 4 speed
Power: 12.3 hp
Top Speed: 72 mph
Weight: 238 lbs
Wheel Size: 3.50 x 10"

21 P150 X

Model Year: 1978
Engine: 149.5 cc, 2 stroke
Transmission: 4 speed
Power: 9 hp
Top Speed: 57 mph
Weight: 229 lbs
Wheel Size: 3.50 x 10"

22 PX150 E

Model Year: 1982
Engine: 149.5 cc, 2 stroke
Transmission: 4 speed
Power: 9 hp
Top Speed: 63 mph
Weight: 213 lbs
Wheel Size: 3.50 x 10"

23 PK 125
Model Year: 1982
Engine: 121 cc, 2 stroke
Transmission: 4 speed
Power: 4.3 hp
Top Speed: 53 mph
Weight: 192 lbs
Wheel Size: 3.00 x 10"

24 PK 50
Model Year: 1983
Engine: 49.8 cc, 2 stroke
Transmission: 4 speed
Power: 1.5 hp
Top Speed: 25 mph
Weight: 154 lbs
Wheel Size: 3.00 x 10"

25 PK 125 Automatica
Model Year: 1984
Engine: 121 cc, 2 stroke
Transmission: automatic
Power: 5.5 hp
Top Speed: 53 mph
Weight: 198 lbs
Wheel Size: 3.00 x 10"

26 PK 50 Automatica
Model Year: 1985
Engine: 49.2 cc, 2 stroke
Transmission: automatic
Power: 1.5 hp
Top Speed: 25 mph
Weight: 187 lbs
Wheel Size: 3.00 x 10"

27 T5 Pole Position
Model Year: 1985
Engine: 123.5 cc, 2 stroke
Transmission: 4 speed
Power: 11 hp
Top Speed: 65 mph
Weight: 247 lbs
Wheel Size: 3.50 x 10"

28 50 Special
Model Year: 1991
Engine: 49.8 cc, 2 stroke
Transmission: 3 speed
Power: 1.4 hp
Top Speed: 25 mph
Weight: 163 lbs
Wheel Size: 3.00 x 10"

29 PK 50 XL Plurimatic
Model Year: 1991
Engine: 49.8 cc, 2 stroke
Transmission: automatic
Power: 1.5 hp
Top Speed: 25 mph
Weight: N.D.
Wheel Size: 3.00 x 10"

30 50 FL2 HP
Model Year: 1994
Engine: 49.8 cc, 2 stroke
Transmission: 4 speed
Power: 2.3 hp
Top Speed: 28 mph
Weight: 196 lbs
Wheel Size: 3.00 x 10"

31 ET4 125
Model Year: 1996
Engine: 49.8 cc, 4 stroke
Transmission: automatic
Power: 10.9 hp
Top Speed: 59 mph
Weight: 229 lbs
Wheel Size: 100/80 x 10"
120/70 x 10"

32 ET2 50
Model Year: 1996
Engine: 49.4 cc, 2 stroke
Transmission: automatic
Power: N.D.
Top Speed: 28 mph
Weight: 202 lbs
Wheel Size: 100/80 x 10"
120/70 x 10"

33 ET2 50 ie
Model Year: 1996
Engine: 49.4 cc, 2 stroke
Transmission: automatic
Power: N.D.
Top Speed: 28 mph
Weight: 202 lbs
Wheel Size: 100/80 x 10"
120/70 x 10"

34 ET4 150
Model Year: 1999
Engine: 150 cc, 4 stroke
Transmission: automatic
Power: 12.5 hp
Top Speed: 60 mph
Weight: 232 lbs
Wheel Size: 100/80 x 10"
120/80 x 10"

35 ET4 50

Model Year: 2000
Engine: 49.9 cc, 4 stroke
Transmission: automatic
Power: N.D.
Top Speed: 28 mph
Weight: 213 lbs
Wheel Size: 100/80 x 10"
            120/70 x 10"

36 PX 150

Model Year: 2001
Engine: 153 cc, 2 stroke
Transmission: 4 speed
Power: 8.7 hp
Top Speed: 57 mph
Weight: 213 lbs
Wheel Size: 3.50 x 10"

37 Granturismo 200

Model Year: 2003
Engine: 198 cc, 4 stroke
Transmission: automatic
Power: 20 hp
Top Speed: 72 mph
Weight: 304 lbs
Wheel Size: 120/70 x 12"
            130/70 x 12"

38 Granturismo 125

Model Year: 2003
Engine: 124 cc, 4 stroke
Transmission: automatic
Power: 15 hp
Top Speed: 63 mph
Weight: 304 lbs
Wheel Size: 120/70 x 12"
            130/70 x 12"

39 LX 125

Model Year: 2005
Engine: 124 cc, 4 stroke
Transmission: automatic
Power: 10.3 hp
Top Speed: 57 mph
Weight: 243 lbs
Wheel Size: 110/70 x 11"
            120/70 x 10"

40 LX 150

Model Year: 2005
Engine: 151 cc, 4 stroke
Transmission: automatic
Power: 11.7 hp
Top Speed: 59 mph
Weight: 243 lbs
Wheel Size: 110/70 x 11"
            120/70 x 10"

41 LX 50 2T

Model Year: 2005

Engine: 49 cc, 2 stroke

Transmission: automatic

Power: N.D.

Top Speed: 28 mph

Weight: 212 lbs

Wheel Size: 110/70 x 11"
            120/70 x 10"

42 GTS 250 ie

Model Year: 2005

Engine: 244 cc, 4 stroke

Transmission: automatic

Power: 122 hp

Top Speed: 76 mph

Weight: 326 lbs

Wheel Size: 120/70 x 12"
            130/70 x 12"

43 LX 50 4T

Model Year: 2005

Engine: 49.9 cc, 4 stroke

Transmission: automatic

Power: N.D.

Top Speed: 30 mph

Weight: 225 lbs

Wheel Size: 110/70 x 11"
            120/70 x 10"

Special Editions

1 Montlhery

Model Year: 1950

Engine: 125 cc, 2 stroke

Transmission: 3 speed

Power: N.D.

Top Speed: 85 mph

Weight: N.D.

Wheel Size: 3.00 x 10"

2 Siluro

Model Year: 1951

Engine: 124.5 cc, 2 stroke

Transmission: 3 speed

Power: 17.2 hp

Top Speed: 106 mph

Weight: N.D.

Wheel Size: 3.00 x 10"

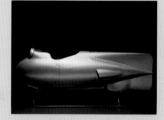

3 Sei Giorni

Model Year: 1951

Engine: 124.2 cc, 2 stroke

Transmission: 3 speed

Power: N.D.

Top Speed: 59 mph

Weight: N.D.

Wheel Size: 3.50 x 8"

List of Vespa Models

Model	Year	Model	Year
V98	1946–47	150 GS	1957
125	1948–50	150 GL	1957–58
125	1950–52	125	1957–58
125	1952–53	150	1957–58
125 "U"	1953	150 GS	1958
125	1953–54	150 GS	1958
150	1954–55	125	1958–59
125	1954–55	150	1958–60
150 GS	1955	150 GS	1959
150	1955–56	150 GL	1959–61
150 GS	1956	125	1959–61
150	1956–57	150 GS	1960
125	1956–57	150	1960–62

Model	Year	Model	Year
150 GS	1961	125	1963–64
125	1961	50 N (small m. door)	1963–65
150 GL	1961–62	50 S	1963–66
125	1961-62	90	1963–84
150 GL	1962	180 SS	1964
150 GS mk 1	1962	160 GS mk 1	1964
160 GS mk 1	1962	150 GL	1964
125	1962–63	125	1964–66
150	1962–67	150 GL	1965
150 GS mk 1	1963	180 SS	1965
160 GS mk 1	1963	125 Primavera	1965–67
160 GS mk 1	1963	50 N (standardized model)	1965–67
150 GL	1963	125 Super	1965–69

Model	Year		Model	Year
50 Super Sprint (SS)	1965–71		180 Rally	1968–73
90 SS	1965–71		50 S (lenghtened wheelbase)	1968–76
150 Sprint	1965–74		125 GTR	1968–78
150 Super	1965–79		50 R	1969–71
180 SS	1966		50 Elestart	1969–72
50 L	1966–67		50 Special	1969–72
50 S (standardized model)	1966–68		150 Sprint Veloce	1969–79
125 GT	1966–73		90 Racer	1971–74
50 L (lenghtened wheelbase)	1967–70		50 Sprinter	1971–79
50 N (lenghtened wheelbase)	1967–71		50 Elestart	1972–75
125 Primavera	1967–83		50 Special	1972–75
180 SS	1968		200 Rally	1972–79
180 SS	1968		50 Elestart (4 speed)	1975–76

Model	Year		Model	Year
125 TS	1975–78		PX 200E Arcobaleno El	1981–90
Primavera ET3	1976–90		PK 125	1982–85
P 200X	1977		PX 200E	1982–86
P 200E	1977–82		PK 125S	1982–86
P125X	1977–82		PK 50 S	1982–86
50 R	1977–84		PK 50	1982–88
50 S	1977–84		AutomaticaPK 125S El	1983–84
50 Special (4 speed)	1977–84		PK 50 SS Elestart	1983–86
P150 X	1978–81		AutomaticaPK 125S	1983–86
100	1978–83		PK 125S Elestart	1983–86
P150 S	1978–90		PK 50 S Elestart	1983–86
PX 125E	1981–83		PK 50 SS	1983–87
PX 150E	1981–85		PX 200E Arcobaleno	1983–90

Model	Year	Model	Year
PX 150E Arcobaleno	1983–90	PK 50 XL Plurimatic El	1986–90
PX 125E Arcobaleno	1983–93	PK 50 XLS	1986–90
AutomaticaPK 50 S	1984	PK 125 XL	1986–90
AutomaticaPK 50 S El	1984–85	PK 50 XLS Plurimatic	1987
PK 125 ETS	1984–85	PK 50 XLS Plurimatic El	1987–89
PX 150E Arcobaleno El	1984–90	PK 125 XL Plurimatic El	1987–90
PX 125E Arcobaleno El	1984–90	Cosa 150	1987–90
PK 50 XL Elestart	1985–90	PK 125 XL Plurimatic	1987–90
PX 125 T5	1985–90	PK 50 XL Rush El	1988
PK 50 XL	1985–90	PK 50 XL Rush	1988–90
PK 50 XL Plurimatic	1986–89	50 N Plurimatic	1989–90
PX 125 T5 Elestart	1986–90	50 N	1989–90
PK 125 XL Elestart	1986–90	125 Automatica	1990

Model	Year		Model	Year
125	1990		PX 150 Kat	2001
125	1990–91		PX 125	2001*
50 Automatica	1990–96		PX 150	2001*
50	1990–94		Granturismo 200	2003*
50 Special	1991		Granturismo 125	2003*
PK 125 Plurimatic	1991–94		LX 150	2005*
50 FL2 HP	1994–96		LX 125	2005*
ET4 125	1996–05		LX 50 2T	2005*
ET2 50	1996–05		LX 50 4T	2005*
ET2 50 ie	1996–05		GTS 250 ie	2005*
ET4 150	1999–05			
ET4 50	2000–05			
PX 125 Kat	2001		* Still in production	

About the author

Valerio Boni was born in Milan on February 23, 1959. He bought his first Vespa 50 in 1974 and started his career in journalism with *Il Pilota Moto* in 1977. He subsequently worked for major Italian motorcycling magazines such as *Motosprint* and *La Moto*. He has been editor of the weekly *Auto Oggi* since 1989. He has ridden over 180,000 miles on Vespa scooters and attended the unveiling of every new model since 1977.